Find Your Authentic Self and Go Fetch It!

IT'S YOUR TURN

*Fun and exciting ways to help you
discover the true you
and create the career you deserve*

Dr. Barbara Collins

*Peace and Blessings,

Dr. Barbara Collins*

IT'S YOUR TURN:
Find Your Authentic Self and Go Fetch It!
by Dr. Barbara Collins

Published by:

Dr. Barbara R. Collins
www.drbarbaracollins.com

Printed in the United States of America

ISBN: 0-9776031-0-5

Editing & book design:

Jack Out of the Box Designs
www.jackoutofthebox.com

Dedication

This book is lovingly dedicated to

My beautiful daughters Monique and Sherri,
who courageously live with passion and purpose.
Thank you for always believing in me.

and

My greatest fan — my life partner Ben
for his support and love.

Foreword

Have you achieved "success," yet sometimes feel empty and wonder if this is all there is?

Do you ever wonder if you're suffering from a mid-life crisis?

Do you tend to take care of everyone else and put yourself last?

Do you want to live a life that really matters; you're just not sure where or how to begin?

If you answered "yes" to any of the above questions, this book is for you.

Dr. Barbara Collins shares specific ways to build the quality of personal and professional life you want, need and deserve . . . now, not someday.

Although she has impressive academic credentials, Dr. Collins doesn't speak like an "ivory tower" professor and she doesn't write a dense, dull textbook full of facts and figures.

It's Your Turn is packed with specific suggestions, thought-provoking insights, laugh-out-loud anecdotes and real-life stories about people just like you who have overcome their fears, doubts and challenges to become the person they've always wanted to be.

If you want to tap into your hidden talents, feel passionately about your work; be pro-active about problems you're facing; call upon your reserves of courage to get out of your comfort zone, take wise risks and develop a more meaningful life; this practical and powerful message is just what the doctor ordered.

You will enjoy Barbara's journey and be inspired to chart your own new path to self-discovery and self-fulfillment. Read it and reap.

— Sam Horn, author/speaker
of *What's Holding You Back?*
and *Tongue Fu!*®
www.samhorn.com

Acknowledgments

Affirming that in God all things are possible, and I am a child of God — loved and cherished.

My mother, father and brother all transitioned from this life over a span of 12 years. I miss them very much. With all their humanness and creativity, I received a legacy of love, tenacity, strength and talents that I treasure each day. I thank them for the lessons of living and surviving in a world that is not always fair.

In writing this book, I experienced my journey to self-discovery. I began writing "It's Your Turn" five years ago. My initial goal was to write a book titled "Career Empowerment Strategies" to help women create a fulfilling career. While conducting "Career Empower Strategies" seminars, I discovered that women needed to feel empowered to take a pause in life to discover their hidden talents and gifts. This is the reason I added two chapters in the book about authenticity. During the seminars, women began to see the importance in taking the time to do the work of self discovery. Many women made the commitment to "Go fetch it." I thank all the women in my seminars who took a risk to share their stories of self-discovery. They gave me energy and enthusiasm to keep doing the work to help women find their true selves. I learned something new from all the women who dared to share their passion, pain and dreams with me. If you attended any of my seminars, wherever you are, I wish you peace and a life of celebrating who you are.

I received incredible motivation to write "It's Your Turn" from my beautiful daughters, Monique and Sherri. I thank Monique and Sherri for witnessing my journey of self-discovery unconditionally. At times, my journey of self-discovery may have appeared self-absorbed, painful and, at times, exciting to my daughters. I thank them both for hanging in there with me in my growth. My daughters are my role models and it is a pleasure to witness their own journey to self-discovery. They both are doing their own inner work and I applaud their strength and sense of purpose.

Judith Jamison, dancer and choreographer, said, "Women are blessed with a jewel of strength that glows all the time." My friends are women who have their own signature glow. Each glow affirmed that I was also writing this book for them. I thank each of them for helping me soar beyond my own belief. Just by saying, "You go girl" or "Wow, you did it!" was an affirmation that I am supported and loved. You each know who you are.

Learning Something New, my Freedom Theatre audition, I will never forget the support I received from Thom Page, director of Community Relations at Freedom Theatre. Thank you, Thom, for helping me fulfill my dream of acting.

My life partner, Ben, came to me as a gift from God. He is my greatest fan. I thank him from the bottom of my heart for believing in me and supporting me in my dreams. We do make a great team and I am so grateful to have Ben in my life.

As a professional speaker and a member of the National Speakers Association, I received tremendous support in writing this book. Kirstin Carey, a colleague and friend, is a remarkable person who shared her talents. Thank you, Kirstin, for helping me break down my writing goals in small chunks and for allowing me to borrow a few quotations from your book, "Out of the Mouths of Babes: PowHERful Quotes by Women with Something to Say." I learned from Kirstin that my dreams don't have to become bigger than I can handle. After experiencing five different editors over a five-year period in writing this book, Kirstin referred me Erin Hyland, my editor.

I thank Erin for understanding my vision in writing this book. Erin, I believe truly, came into my life in writing this book at the right time. It was affirming to read her comments after reading my manuscript. Now I know what it means to never, never, never give up. Erin's knowledge and expertise in making my book happen I will treasure.

The many members in NSA and the local chapter, MAC, too numerous to mention by name, supported me and encouraged me to keep moving forward with my goals. I cherish my connection with NSA. I learned the craft and skills to make my dreams come true. I thank all my friends from NSA who touched my life at local meetings and national conferences — Mark LeBlanc, thank you for validating my gift of speaking and giving unconditional acceptance in my growth and development; Sam Horn, the greatest visionary who gave me the title "It's Your Turn"; Marjorie Brody, who introduced me to NSA; and Jovita Jenkins, for answering my questions about writing her first book, "Getting Out of Your Own Way."

All of my life, I have trusted in God that my purpose in life would be revealed. I am clear about my purpose and it is such a joy knowing that at this time of my life. I am grateful for God's anonymous angels who lovingly guided me and kept me on the path of authenticity. One of my mother's favorite songs is "When I have Done the Best I Can." The words to the song are a peaceful reminder that when my journey is over - I will know that I have done the best I could.

TABLE OF CONTENTS

INTRODUCTION

"Expecting life to treat you well because you are a good person is like expecting an angry bull not to charge because you are a vegetarian."

– *Shari R. Barr, author and businesswoman*

Legend has it that the symbol of the Sankofa bird originates from the word "Sankofa," which in the Akan language means to go back to the past in order to build for the future.

Sankofa is symbolic of the spiritual mindset and cultural awakening of African people in the decades of their independence. Though the concept may seem new, it is an old tradition that links people to the discovery of their past, which is a fundamental building block for the future.

The Sankofa bird is characterized by the turning of its head in the direction of its tail. In reality, the bird is either removing something from its tail, searching through its tail feathers or grooming itself. The Akan likens this action to looking backward, a symbol of looking at one's past, or with the quest for knowledge, returning to the source.

Looking back in order to move forward empowers you to discover your authenticity, affirm your talents and own your power. This book is meant to act as your Sankofa bird on your journey to discovering your authentic self.

When I took this journey, I returned to my past to discover the real me. It was as if I was in a dark tunnel, and everything I needed to know was outside waiting to be discovered. Any new experience I learned about the new me felt like sudden beams of light flashing in the tunnel. The brighter the light, the more I was able to see my God-given talents.

Have you ever experienced a sudden burst of light hitting your eyes? Initially, the light hurts your eyes until they adjust. This is how I felt when I discovered different parts of my authenticity. When I emerged from the dark tunnel of not knowing myself, what I saw was amazing. Through self-discovery, I uncovered revelations I had never imagined. It all began with a dim light of awareness that grew brighter and brighter.

The tunnel is a metaphor for uncovering the unknown after wandering in the dark. The light is symbolic of the empowerment of true self. When we find ourselves on life's journey to rediscover, we all look for that dim light.

Author Elisabeth Kubler-Ross has said, "People are like stained-glass windows. They sparkle and shine when the sun is out, but when the darkness sets in, their true beauty is revealed only if there is a light from within."

If part of something important is missing, the Sankofa legend tells us it is wise to "go back and fetch it," thus, return to the beginning or retrace our steps to find parts of the missing solution. Sankofa is the repossession of something forgotten and the initiation of returning to the place where the object was lost in order to fetch it and move forward.

"It's Your Turn" will help you to rediscover your purpose in life. Perhaps you selected this book or maybe a friend bought it for you. It really doesn't matter how it came into your life. If you are willing to participate in these career empowerment strategies, you will gain the courage to look inside yourself and create the career you deserve. I did it for myself. In fact, I continue to do it every day.

For me, understanding the concept of "Sankofa" was a pivotal moment that convinced me that it was my turn to find my authentic self. Another came as I was reading Katheleen A. Brehony's book, Awakening at Midlife. In the book, she describes the thoughts of Abraham Maslow and Carl Jung, two of my favorite behaviorists on human growth and development. "Like Maslow," Brehony says, "Jung believed that the purpose of life was the unfolding of the unique, individual inner core or 'self' that is inherent in every person."

This is what I want for you. I want you to say, "It's my turn to become all that I can become." For many, women especially, finding their authentic self may seem daunting or self-serving. Saying "It's Your Turn" is a way to pause and reflect on how to be more than you think you are.

If you need reasons to take a pause, here are a few I hope will spur you on to do your inner work.

"It's Your Turn" because:

- *You deserve to create the life you want.*
- *You deserve to know the truth about who you are – and have faith that whatever you find is all good.*
- *You are more than you think you are.*
- *You are worth doing the work of finding self.*

- *You know, deep down inside, no one can do this work but you.*

- *You can create a support team if you need help to rediscover your true self.*

- *You do not have to do this alone. (Your Spiritual source, or guiding higher power will always be with you. If you decide to get therapeutic help it does not mean you are mentally unstable – you just need a little help.)*

- *You will look authentically beautiful, balanced, and in sync with the universe.*

Convinced? I say, "It's Your Turn to Go Fetch It! "

Empowerment is worthwhile and exciting. Discovering who you are creates a better you, and it empowers you to make positive and authentic career decisions. There is a light inside of you; let it begin to shine brightly and commence your journey to empowerment.

This book differs from many self-help career books. Few career books recognize that the most critical stage in selecting a career is uncovering one's authenticity. Discovering your authenticity can be a daunting experience as we are unsure of what we will find. You are not alone in fighting negative self-messages that limit uncovering the gems inside of you. This book focuses on our positive images that are either hidden or suppressed as a result of life's experiences.

This book contains ideas and experiences of people I met in my Career Empowerment Strategies workshops. It is dedicated to those workshop participants who persistently requested more information about Career Empowerment Strategies.

These strategies are filled with creative ways to discover your career passion. Creative Career Empowerment Strategies provides a five-step approach to help you design your career path:

- *Understanding Authenticity*
- *Discovering Your Authenticity*
- *Creating a Career Vision*
- *Creating a Career Portfolio*
- *Networking, Networking, Networking*

You may have 20, 30 or even 40 career years ahead of you; it doesn't matter how many you have. What is important is that identifying and discovering your authenticity helps rediscover the person you neglected due to life's demands and detours. Taking the time to discover your authentic self is a wonderful experience. At first, this might feel overwhelming. Don't worry; this is normal! Remember, delving into uncharted territory for the first time is daunting. Don't give up; you will soon feel like a new person.

Creating a career vision stems from the quote, "What the mind can conceive the mind can achieve." Mental-visioning prepares the mind for success. And, gathering written evidence of talents and gifts is the purpose in designing a career portfolio strategy.

Networking connects your authenticity, vision, knowledge, talents and skills to resources that support your career journey. Networking creates results by placing in the universe your creative intentions. Watch what happens when you meet someone through networking. Inevitably, someone will link right into your career path or provide you with the information you need. All of the steps in the Career Empowerment Strategies are important, but networking creates the energy needed for the universe to set your career journey in motion.

While I was on my career journey, I found many hidden gems. I am grateful to my Divine Spirit, the creator who guided and empowered me with the courage to look within and develop a deserving career. Self-examination was difficult at first, but with prayer and affirmation that the Spirit loves me, I was encouraged to face all I needed to know about my past and present.

You are a unique and special person with gems buried deep inside you. Let's uncover those riches for the world to see. You may be hesitant to look inside yourself or perhaps you have forgotten your role in life. Or, maybe you are dissatisfied with your job. Whatever the reason, enjoy the journey. We have been connected with the Spirit.

CHAPTER 1

UNDERSTANDING AUTHENTICITY

> "Always be a first-rate version of yourself,
> instead of a second-rate version of somebody else."
>
> — *Judy Garland*

Discovering your authenticity is the first step in designing your career. But, first, you must understand its importance. You will discover, rediscover and/or reacquaint yourself with your true identity — your passion, your likes, dislikes, values, strengths, challenges and talents. Sounds like a lot, doesn't it?

Most likely, a lot within you is hidden. You might think you will uncover the negative instead of the positive attributes about your self. What if you flip the negative thoughts and say, "If I look inward, will I discover wonderful things about me and accept the negative challenges that made me who I am today, strong and determined?"

My journey to discovering my authenticity began on a warm,

summer night inside Philadelphia's Freedom Theatre, one of the oldest African-American theaters in the country. I was attending my daughter's graduation performance titled, "Moments of Sharing." She was wonderful, and, of course, I was a very proud mother. During the performance, one of the adult student-actors recited a poem titled, "Who Am I?"

I cried after listening to the powerful words. I felt empty inside, almost as if I was falling through a deep, dark empty tunnel, unable to save myself. It hit me; I really didn't know who I was.

Yes, I was a single mother, daughter, teacher and a friend, but there was more to me. I wanted to know why God put me on this earth. What was I to do? What was my purpose in life? I know I am not an accident in the divine planning of life. As a mother, I was grateful to be raising two daughters alone while working successfully in my career. But that night at the theatre, I realized I had put my inner life on hold.

My experience at Freedom Theatre released a huge "a-ha" freeing revelation. I knew probing deeper within was necessary to discover the real me. Hidden talents nurturing since birth now led me on a different path.

 I prayed for strength while performing the demanding roles of single mother, teacher, friend and daughter. Raising my two beautiful daughters, Sherri and Monique, was challenging, yet packed with proud moments of joy as I watched them evolve into beautiful young women.

Yet, I felt out of sync and empty. I filled this emptiness in all the wrong ways. I acquired materials things. I worked three jobs so that by day's end I would not have to reflect. Instead, I could just fall into bed exhausted. For me, hard work was the payoff that I was a good person. I judged success by how hard I worked and exceeded the expectations of my corporate position. I was on automatic pilot.

I was climbing the career ladder in a major corporation when I experienced my "a-ha" moment at Freedom Theatre. As the manager of a training and development department, I was visible and very successful. I paid my dues. I experienced overt racism and sexism to the Nth degree. As a former fourth-grade teacher, I was naive about the ruthlessness occurring in corporate America.

I attended a conference for human-resource professionals and organizational-development consultants. One workshop in particular confirmed my discomfort in working in a corporate environment. The purpose of the workshop was to identify your creativity level and perception of the corporate structure. We took an inventory instrument to assess our creative quotient. Scores ranged from 0 (a structured perception of a corporate environment) to 149 (the most unstructured perception of the corporate environment). I scored 148, which indicated that I perceived no walls, barriers or boundaries in the corporate world. This explained why I felt like a square peg in a round hole.

After the workshop, the trainer and I spoke. He suggested that although I was very successful in my managerial role, I might feel out of sync and not enjoy my work. He was absolutely correct.

Coincidentally, perhaps, this workshop was toward the end of my 10th year in the corporation and it helped me to begin the self-discovery necessary to move on in my career.

During this time, I was also experiencing a difficult and painful divorce impacting my self-esteem. Divorce was a sign of failure, and its reality plunged me into deep crevices of depression. I went to work feeling numb and empty. Losing too much weight, I knew I had to do something to keep my sanity. God was my co-pilot, and through the power of prayer I survived. A friend told me that that she remembers seeing me walking downtown, tears steaming down my face, not acknowledging anyone or even caring if anyone saw me. The nightmarish hell of moving through the grief of an ending marriage is difficult to explain unless you have experienced divorce yourself. What I did not realize at the time was that by avoiding the pain of emptiness, I was digging a deeper hole.

Hearing the poem "Who Am I?" at Freedom Theatre reminded me that it was time to uncover the layers of who I am. The roles were no longer enough. At that time, I was unaware of what awaited me, but I remembered that I had lofty dreams and goals at one time in my life. Most of all, I knew I was creative.

Rebecca Maddox, in her book "Inc. Your Dreams," wrote, "Finding out who you are is like going on an archaeological dig."

Discovering your authentic self is hard work, but worth every minute. It is an evolving process requiring time and patience.

When we are born, we bring gifts into this world. Along the way, our gifts can remain unopened or can be torn apart or damaged. This leads to resentful feelings of anger and awkwardness in a world that does not provide what we need to feel whole.

The Freedom Theatre experience was a major turning point in my life. I made a commitment to recreate my teen-age experiences by being totally engaged in a life doing what I enjoyed. Deepak Chopra, the author of "The Seven Spiritual Laws of Success," describes this feeling as being in your dharma; doing what you love while the hours seem mindless.

This was exactly what I needed to find. I knew my career

journey would not happen by waiting for someone or something else.

Returning to my past meant talking to my relatives about my family history and ancestors. Their stories helped me to reconnect to the strength and character embedded in my genes.

My grandmother told me that my grandfather helped to build the Panama Canal. Sadly, he was paid in silver while the Europeans were paid in gold. My grandmother said I inherited a legacy of survival, determination and fortitude. A long line of West Indian and southern black relatives passed this on to me.

I planned our family reunion with my cousin in Barbados to create our family tree. During our laughing and catching up on family gossip, Dennis showed me photos of my relatives. One picture was of my great-grandfather, who was Scottish. The photo showed a stern Caucasian man, looking very regal with a long white mustache. I was shocked when I saw the picture.

I knew that my grandparents' last name "Bailey" was a Scottish derivative, but I was still taken aback to learn my lineage was partly white. I cannot imagine what my great-grandmother must have been like during the early 1800s, but I can only assume that she was either in love with my great-grandfather or captured by his dominance as a slave owner. The latter assumption was most likely the reality. However, I prefer to leave my thoughts open and just embrace that their union created nine sons, one being my grandfather, Lambert Bailey.

Discovering your authenticity in order to create the career you deserve is not for the faint of heart. It takes courage and faith to look deeper to find those positive attributes and wonderful characteristics you once had in your life. It can be painful at times, but when you come to see the beauty inside of you, people will notice your power and the light will shine through your eyes.

Today, after many years of self-discovery, and still on this road, I am beginning to feel more complete and authentic. I got sidetracked somewhere in my life and wandered in the dark.

Looking inward was not on my agenda. I rationalized that I had no time; I was too busy raising children and being a wife. Fortunately, following the Freedom Theatre experience, I began reading more about self-esteem and being in the Spirit, along with anything else that would assist me in my journey of rediscovery.

Perhaps you didn't experience a revelation or a pivotal moment like me. Or maybe you haven't given much consideration to authentic self-revelation. To spark your thoughts and change any negative ideas around finding your authenticity, you should try career empowerment strategies.

Now that you are clear about the value of self-discovery and readiness for change, let's share some of the activities that make discovering who you are fun and exciting. You may find some of the strategies uncomfortable or even strange. You may be inspired to create your own activities as part of the process of uncovering your authenticity. Just try one to see what happens. Remember, no action means lack of results.

IT'S YOUR TURN (activity)

READINESS FOR SELF-DISCOVERY: Before you begin discovering your authenticity, take a break, stop reading this and get a sheet paper. Write down all of your talents and skills in 15 seconds. Don't cheat; ask someone to time you to keep you honest.

How many did you write? If you wrote more than 10, you are well on your way to discovering your authenticity. When I ask people in my workshops to do this, inevitably they find it challenging to write more than five.

Once, after a workshop, a participant shared with me that my empowerment stories helped her recall comments from friends, complimenting her on traits that she ignored or took for granted. She realized that she needed to work on acceptance of who she was and honor the wonderful things about herself.

Within each of us are many talents and skills we suppressed because of detours that appeared in life. These activities will help you begin the archaeological dig to your past and uncover the gems buried inside. So, "Go fetch it!"

DISCOVERING YOUR AUTHENTICITY

"You only live once – but if you work it right, once is enough."

— Joe E. Lewis

Rounding Up The Old Crew

I rounded up my old high school friends, my "cut" buddies as I called them, in one activity to discover my authentic self. These were friends who spent hours with me on the phone, the ones who I thought knew me better than my parents. I even called my first real boyfriend. I thought meeting with these high school buddies and asking for feedback on the positive things they remembered about me would help me on my mission to discover my authentic self.

This proved a great activity because the feedback was from good friends who knew me during a time when I was not distracted with adult responsibilities. Prior to contacting them, I created a few important ground rules.

Ground Rules

- *Give only positive feedback. (I wanted the meeting to be fun.)*

- *Remember this is not a therapy session. No solving problems.*

- *Keep the conversation focused on the mission, then let my friends join the sharing session. (This may sound self-serving, but it is very easy to get distracted, especially because I had not seen my friends in a long time. I remembered that I created this activity with good friends who understand and are supportive to me.)*

- *Only an hour on my issues. (I did not want my friends to think the entire meeting was focused on me.)*

- *Select the perfect place to gather. Great restaurants always work. Or, create a home-cooked, soul-food dinner. (I took a risk in getting my old friends together to create this meeting for me. But I felt my journey to discovering me was worth the risk. Besides, this was a good reason to reconnect.)*

We met at a quaint New Orleans-type restaurant on the east side in New York City. The ambiance was warm and cozy with large, white, ornately decorated high-back chairs at large round tables. This was an intimate setting for the sharing of old stories and laughing about the good old days.

During dinner, David, my first boyfriend, surprised me with a story I had never heard. He said, "Do you remember our first date? We went to a movie, but before we left, your father asked you to run a quick errand for him, down the street to a neighbor's house. While you were gone, he said he wanted to have a chat with me. You probably would have been devastated if you knew the conversation was about you."

David was right; I was 16 and trying to create an image of sophistication and maturity.

David continued, "Your father, politely asked what my intentions were with his daughter." My father was apprehensive about our relationship because my father thought David was too old for me. He was 18.

David recalled my father answering the door the first time he came to take to me out. He was wearing all black and dark sunglasses. Your father opened the door and said, "You must be visiting me as old as you look."

My father was gentle and kind, but this issue of dating his daughter was serious. I laughed very hard upon hearing this surprise confession from David.

He continued, "Your father said he had every intention of his daughter attending college next year, and he did not expect any disruption in that goal." David knew my dad meant business when he told him he would want to explore uncharted waters with other girls.

David said he liked and respected my father, and respected me, so he decided to move on to date a friend of mine.

I recall how devastated I was when we broke up, but I never knew why. I had been jealous, angry and questioned my attractiveness. And, my father never told me that story. What a relief when David gave me the answer to an unknown. We laughed and exchanged comments of coming to closure. David said my father left a lasting impression on him early in his life.

David remained friends with my family and, ironically, years later ran into my father in New York. Then, they started their own friendship.

After listening to David's story, I remembered my father as quiet. He did not demonstrate his emotions often. He worked long hours constantly, unable to spend as much quality time with me as I wanted. He was almost like an absent father. David's story affirmed for me that my dad cared and loved me very much, and I needed to hear that. I started creating a vision of my father involved in my life in his own way.

I called my father immediately after the dinner to ask if he remembered that conversation. He chuckled and said, "Of course I do. I just wanted David to be clear about his intentions with you. You ended up going to college, and that was my point."

Well, enough said. My father's message was clear.

Although David's story did not reveal any particular skill or specific talent I had, it more importantly gave me a gift. It made me realize my father's love for me. What better way to begin my journey in self-discovery?

My friend Diane recalled how I loved to give parties. She remembered how I could find any excuse for a party — birthdays, good grades or graduation. She admired how I organized the parties and easily delegated tasks for everyone. I transferred those skills to my current work experience; I know how to plan, delegate and implement a project. My organizational skills in partying paid off!

 Sharon laughed about my passion to perform in school plays and the school chorus. Our school plays could be corny, but Sharon recalled that that didn't matter to me. Give me a stage and I was on it. Now I know why I love professional speaking.

My hour was completed, and I must admit it was hard to stop hearing about myself. The conversation was contagious. Dinner continued with my friends recalling their own memories of themselves. Meeting with them was enlightening. I was highly motivated to move forward in my quest of finding the real authentic me.

IT'S YOUR TURN (activity)

ROUND UP YOUR OLD CREW: Calling old friends may feel awkward at first, especially if you are uncomfortable reaching out to people. Once you move through the initial fear, though, many possibilities await you. The secret to feeling comfortable in rounding up the old crew is selecting trusting and positive friends who have your best interest at heart. Selecting someone you dated may work for you too. It was not uncomfortable for me to call David because we remained friends for many years later. What matters is leaving yourself open to hearing exciting, and possibly surprising, information about yourself.

You may not be comfortable reaching back into your past to find a group of friends. An alternative to this strategy will help you accomplish your goals without involving a group of people.

MEET ONE-ON-ONE: The purpose of this activity is to meet with an old schoolmate or friend to solicit feedback on your talents and skills forgotten throughout your life journey. This activity is designed to reconnect you to your past and to begin unleashing some of that passion from your earlier years. This is a great "Go fetch it" experience.

Ask one friend from high school, an old friend or a family member — someone who you trust — to partner with you. Ask your partner to meet and help you remember your positive traits. It might help to select someone who you have recently connected with over the years to avoid a shocking response to your request. One-on-one contact provides an opportunity to discuss your history more intimately. The setting for your meeting could be in a restaurant, a bookstore or some other place equally comfortable for both. Pick a place that removes the formality from the conversation.

Remember these ground rules:

- *Ask for positive feedback.*

- *No solving problems. This is not a therapy session to meet your needs.*

- *Keep the conversation focused on you, then set aside time for sharing with your partner.*

- *An hour should be long enough for your mission.*

- *Thank your partner and say the lunch/dinner is on you.*

Ask your partner to describe your positive attributes in one-word phrases, such as "friendly" or "kind." Select one of the words from this list and ask your partner to share thoughts on why he/she selected that particular word. For example, if you selected "passionate," ask how you demonstrated passion. You may suggest your partner make a list prior to the meeting. Either option depends on your comfort zone with him/her.

Sharing stories or anecdotes about your past with someone is another way to find out more about the real you. This is a great opportunity to sift out specific interests or skills that you demonstrated. Many stories are fun to hear, but sometimes you may share stories that produce sad memories. Don't pull back from these sad stories unless they are too painful. Your partner may be trying to indicate that during that particularly difficult time, you demonstrated a positive attribute worth remembering. For example, your partner may recall a time when a family member experienced a difficult moment in his/her life. He/she may say this was a time when you demonstrated leadership, compassion or strength.

Stories are evidences of our history that many times go untold among a circle of friends or family. Take this opportunity to listen to your partner tell your story; you may be surprised.

Remember the story my first boyfriend told me in the
"Rounding Up the Old Crew" activity? While discussing your
talents and skills, you may find that the conversation turns into a
two-way discussion. This is fine as long as the conversation is
focused on meeting your expectations. If the conversation starts
drifting to your partner, that's fine too. Remember these
activities are contagious. Just politely say to your partner, "If you
don't mind, it will be easier for me to take all this information in
if we take turns doing the exercise." If you have selected
someone who cares about you, this will not be a problem.

Get Out of Your Comfort Zone

After you hear about your forgotten skills and talents, it's time
to test the waters of discovery.

"Discovering Your Authenticity" means getting out of your
comfort zone and pushing the envelope to make something
different happen in your life. Getting out of your comfort zone
means looking at life as an adventure to discover more about
you. It is the archaeological dig that helps you discover who
you are with added excitement to the process. These activities
will challenge you to reveal hidden talents.

Stretch yourself to experiment with new activities, such as
something you always thought about doing, but were afraid to
try. This career-empowerment strategy helps to peel off another
layer in discovering who you are.

For example, you may discover in meeting with old friends that
you are good at roller-skating. Now this may not lead to a
career choice, but it does give you an added feeling of
accomplishment. If you remembered that you enjoyed hiking,
group travel tours are great for opening up new experiences
and connecting to a passion.

Or you could try spelunking, an adventure that put me way out of my comfort zone.

I enrolled in a master's degree program during the late '70s that required taking an advanced group analysis course. I recalled this story years later because it impacted my life by uncovering new information about me.

This two-week course in Bushkill, predominantly a forest and bush area in the Pennsylvania mountains, was conducted by a young professor fresh out of graduate school. He explained that the course was designed to teach physical intervention strategies for doing group process work. The purpose of this activity was to assess our leadership styles and to analyze how groups function and how the members interact with each other.

As I was unfamiliar with the terminology, a classmate whispered that we were going cave climbing. I knew this was going to be an adventure that would really stretch my comfort zone.

For three days, all I thought about was the cave. My emotions were mixed with concern, fear and excitement. The day arrived and, after donning my spelunking gear, I felt like I was going on a safari. The professor provided little information about the trip.

I kept thinking to myself that there must be another way to get through this course. Did I really pay all this money just to go through a cave? En-route to the cavern, our instructor showed us a beautiful waterfall. At the bottom were cold cans of refreshing beer and soda. "This is what will be waiting for us after we have completed our quest," he said.

While listening to the professor's instructions, I remember staying close to my classmate Fred. He was 6 feet tall and had a protective look, and I thought I would need him in the cave. He proved to be a wonderful partner.

As we entered the cave, it felt cold and damp. It was dark inside and crawling was a challenge. At times, I could barely hold my head up. And, at one point, I could not see my hand in front of me. The group helped and supported each other, but emotions escalated as we inched through the cave.

At first, I was not the model student. An hour inside the cave, I fussed and complained that I did not want to be there. It was dark, wet and very hot, and I know I saw a few bats flying around. I kept asking myself, "Why am I doing this?"

A couple of hours in the cave, we stopped at an open area that was very dark. The instructor asked the group to express their feelings. Classmates started to reveal sides of themselves that I had not detected from prior program courses. When faced with a challenge, it is amazing what thoughts come to mind. I remember thinking about my children, and how much they depended on me to prepare them for young adulthood.

The turning point for me occurred about four hours in the cave. Although we followed instructions and were determined to complete the experience, some in the group were ready to form a mutiny. There I was with 20 strangers, wondering out loud why I had paid such high tuition for the course. These comments were mild compared to those expressed by my colleagues.

I continued to climb through the cave, many times on my stomach. There was another woman in front of me. Behind me was the classmate who stood more than 6 feet tall. He comforted me in the beginning, when I was feeling unconfident and did not believe we would ever get out.

About four hours in, though, I felt no fear. Rather, I felt confident that we were, in fact, getting out of this cave. I trusted those around me, and even offered to help others who needed assistance. While climbing, I was focused on helping those people deal with their fear and frustration.

Our instructor guided us through the first half of the adventure. He remained at the end of the line on our way back out. While crawling out, someone suggested that we return without light. I supported the challenge, being caught up in the moment. I wanted to see if we could really do this.

This challenge, however, was not well accepted by one group member. As the group moved on, she yelled, "I refuse to climb any farther without any light."

We were all exhausted and wanted to get out of the cave. Our instructor took advantage of this time to process our decisions within the group. I noticed that we had begun to challenge him and push the boundaries within the group as we became more comfortable and trusting of each other. Most of us weren't sure what to do because we could not move. We participated in an interactive group discussion in the cave anyway.

The result of our discussion was to use light as we returned. Moreover, the current leader in the cave decided that she did not want to lead anymore; so, the group asked for volunteers. Guess who volunteered?

Yes, I did.

Why I did I now understand. In times of crisis, I try to help in any way I can. When a situation becomes challenging, I take over and do what is necessary to solve the problem. I think raising children and teaching elementary school prepared me for crisis situations. I put myself on automatic pilot and perform without fear.

After five hours, we emerged from the cave successfully. After several discussions in the cave, and with group support, we succeeded in meeting our goal.

As we ended our long, hot and scary journey out of the dark, we found the beer, soda and all the food that we could eat. We were all so thrilled that we made it out, and our bonds became stronger. We were patting each other on the back and hugging. One group member said, "Hey, Barbara, I knew you could lead us out. You were great." Everyone seemed to verbalize their confidence in my leadership.

I appreciated everyone's comments, but we worked together as a team, supporting each other. Leading everyone out of the cave was my choice to help us achieve our goal.

The group's vote of confidence began to impact me strongly.

Internalizing my emotions, I sat alone on a rock and tried to process my feelings. Larry, my instructor, came over and asked what was wrong. He commented on my excellent leadership skills and assumed that I would feel good about my role in our adventure. I explained that although I felt supported by the group, I felt I was being taken for granted.

He reinforced how I had helped and supported those people who felt lost. He noted how the members were expressing their grateful feelings toward me. I believed everyone was congratulating me because they expected me to be strong, and that I volunteered because no one else would.

I needed just as much validation as anyone else in our group, I realized. He asked how much more validation I needed, and we continued to talk. Larry helped me to understand something about myself. He told me that people created perceptions about me based on what they saw and their own experiences. What people see is their reality.

"Your group saw you as a strong leader. Did you want them to see you any other way," he asked. "Yes, of course, you were afraid, but you were also courageous. Why don't you want people to see your strength?

"Maybe you have difficulty in owning your power."

He said I demonstrated power and communicated leadership, but suggested I wanted people to see something in me that wasn't true. "You want others to sympathize with you," he said.

That statement hit me hard.

What I learned many years after that cave experience is that being authentic means acknowledging the gift of leadership and power that God has given to me. I need to be what people see in me.

I've asked myself why I needed people to see me as fearful rather than courageous. During the cave experience, I was going through my difficult divorce, raising two daughters and completing my master's degree while working a full-time job. Deep inside, I wanted people to feel sorry for me.

It was hard to admit that I did not own my power. My instructor's words stung, but going through that experience brought to the surface information about me that I did not know. I later learned that I am strong, courageous and not afraid to take risks. Yes, leading the group through the cave was challenging, but I needed affirmation that could only come from within myself.

Years after the spelunking experience, I ran into my instructor and reminded him about the cave. He laughed and remarked, "Don't remind me; I was a bit too adventurous as a young professor."

But, I was glad to have gone through it. The cave experience was a solid physical intervention strategy design that challenged us to process our group dynamics. And many times, a cave experience can bring out deep interpersonal issues in members that can create life-changing experiences.

IT'S YOUR TURN (activity)

GET OUT OF YOUR COMFORT ZONE: You may not want to go spelunking, but I'm sure you can find an enjoyable physical activity that gets you out of your comfort zone. Find something you can do with friends or strangers that challenges you to surface the gems buried inside of you.

After one of my workshops, a woman shared her experience about her trip to the Amazon with me. I was impressed with her interest in spending time in a place that most people find challenging. She said the trip validated that she is more than she thinks she is. Proving her authenticity about strength and purpose was her greatest reward. Prior to the trip, she said she had forgotten that she was strong. But the Amazon was the place where she would have to depend on herself for survival. As a result, she looks at challenges differently today.

Taking a trek to the Amazon may not be your idea of empowerment, but adventure empowerment strategies challenge you to reach deep down inside, connecting you to your inner strength and values. Getting out of your comfort zone may add on another layer to affirm who you are in this world and your purpose in life.

In my travels, I meet men and women who want contentment and happiness in life. Life is what you make it, and only you can make what you want to happen actually happen. Prior to my journey to empowerment, I resented the fact that no one was going to rescue me and change my world. After, I realized that changing was going to be my responsibility. Getting out of my comfort zone began to free me from the past and help me to live in the present.

Learn Something New

While consulting with an educational institution in Philadelphia, and I met an 85-year-old man on the board whom I will never forget. He was energetic and demonstrated an enormous quest for living. One day I asked him how he stayed so young at heart. "I learn something new every day," he said.

Learning Something New helps you to not only discover your authentic self, the activity is a proactive way to keep you feeling youthful.

Remember my Rounding Up the Old Crew strategy? One of the comments that stood out for me was my love for acting in plays. Because my friends helped me to remember my interests in acting, I enrolled in an acting course at Freedom Theatre.

This was one of the most difficult decisions I had every made. It may not sound like a life-changing decision, but at that time in my life, I was dragging myself out of a hole of low self-esteem, experiencing a difficult divorce and being a single parent. However, I was determined to find the real me. I knew there was something good about me underneath all my pain and emptiness.

I called Director of Admissions Thom Page, a friend of mine, to ask him if I could audition for the summer acting program. He was thrilled that I was pursuing my love of acting.

When we met, he gave me the monologue to rehearse for my audition. I was shocked when I read it. The character was a prostitute, and I couldn't see myself memorizing the lines. Thom said that the monologue would challenge me to see if I really wanted to act.

Prior to the audition for the course, I was terrified to do something totally out of my comfort zone. I repeatedly phoned a friend to say, "I can't do this." She encouraged me to move through the fear. I knew that acting was a lost passion that needed rekindling. The last time I acted was in high school, and images of failure to humiliation filled my head.

I called Thom a week before the audition to cancel. His administrative assistant told me that Thom could not be reached and suggested that I show up for the audition. Little did I know at the time that Thom had planned all that.

Thom remembered that 15 years earlier, when my daughter was taking acting lessons at Freedom Theatre, he constantly heard me say how much I wanted to learn to act.

After a lot of procrastination and tears, I decided I had no choice. I prayed to God for courage in helping me continue my path of self-discovery.

Before the audition, I asked four close friends to help me practice. While reciting the words to them, I noticed how they focused on every word I was saying. I remember hearing my voice escalate at certain points in the monologue and found myself suddenly immersed in the words I was once afraid to recite.

When I finished, my friends were astonished at how my voice and look changed once I got into character. They didn't understand my nervousness; they told me I did really well. I knew how important it was to have supportive friends while on a journey to find my authenticity.

Then I went to the audition. Sitting next to young children waiting for my turn, I felt humbled. I kept thinking, "What if I forget the words?" So, I reflected on a powerful quote to help me through. "Feel the fear and do it anyway."

When it was my turn, I nervously recited my monologue before several acting instructors. It was not perfect, but I did it. To be honest, I rather enjoyed it.

And, I was accepted into the course! I was so excited to get over the first hurdle toward my goal.

I met interesting and creative people in the acting class. It was held three nights a week, with long hours rehearsing. The time felt endless as I rediscovered a joy suppressed from my past. Learning to act was thrilling.

In reality, acting experience is nothing like spelunking, but it sure felt like it to me. I confronted my fear and received good grades. And, the renewed self-confidence was thrilling. I learned more about the real me. I found new skills that were buried for many years. Taking the classes felt therapeutic. The fear of trying something out of my comfort zone was real, but I did it anyway and moved through my archaeological dig to discover the real me.

I feel fortunate that my "Rounding Up The Crew" dinner surfaced these wonderful memories because with a renewed sense of self-confidence and newfound information about me, I persisted with my journey of self-discovery. I continued taking acting lessons.

A few years later, my daughter Monique and my friend Kimberly spurred me to take the next step. They encouraged me to get involved in TV commercials and print modeling. I was flattered, but apprehensive. "At my age?" I asked.

My daughter saw an opportunity for me to apply my love of performing as another layer in my career journey, and I was ready for the challenge.

Someone once told me that when you are navigating uncharted territory, the first step is the hardest one.

I did not know where to begin. Because my daughter and Kimberly were both involved in acting, they were my support coaches guiding me along the way. Motivational speaker Les Brown has said, "When you need faith in yourself, just ride on someone else's faith in you." So, I rode on Monique's and Kimberly's faiths each step in my new Learning Something New experience.

I made an appointment with a photographer to have headshots taken for my portfolio. The next step was presenting my portfolio to various casting agents.

Following several interviews, three casting agents accepted me as a client. My first casting call found me among many other aspiring actors. I waited patiently for my turn to be interviewed by an advertising agency. As my name was called, I nervously entered the room. The agents sat in a row, all dressed in black, looking like stereotypical New Yorkers. One agent said, "Just tell us who you are."

How interesting that he said that, considering I was already on my own quest to find out who I really was.

I gave them my best description of me, and when I mentioned my age, they looked shocked. The agents gave me kudos for looking so great at my age with two young adult daughters.

My first audition left me feeling positive about myself. I thought I did well. But I knew from my classes that it was best not to project overconfidence in the competitive entertainment industry. The advice I received was to pat myself on the back and move on to the next audition.

Surprisingly, my agent called me the next day and said that I booked my first national print ad. I did not know what the word "booking" meant. She explained that it meant I got the job. My mouth fell open.

The job was to model an older healthy woman who appears to take risks. I was representing a national well-known athletic shoe company, and the creative art director mentioned that my picture would appear in brand stores across the country.

I did not realize the impact of the ad until one day while walking in a shopping mall. I wasn't looking for the ad, but there it was smack in front of me in a full billboard in a store.

After the initial shock, I went in the store to ask if I could have an extra copy. They were excited to see the real person in the ad show up in their store, and I tasted fame for a few minutes. I must admit it felt good. They gave me a copy of the picture and sample promotion boxes. What a thrill this was for me. Thanks to my daughter and Kimberly for believing in me and helping me to "Go fetch it!"

I continue auditioning and, fortunately, I have appeared in several movies, print and TV spots. Currently, I book print ads for major advertising agencies. None of this would have happened if I had not taken a risk and made something happen in my life.

I oversaw pre-admission counseling in Continuing Education for Women at Temple University in Philadelphia during the early '70s. I counseled almost 400 women in one year who were returning to college after a long separation from education. Rewarding experiences came from watching women challenge themselves to rekindle their educational goals.

One 70-year-old woman who came to my office for pre-admission counseling shared her experiences and passion for learning. Her age was no barrier; she had a passion in learning. She believed that in another 10 years, she could accomplish her dream in pursuing an undergraduate degree.

Her energy was contagious. Many times when I was feeling drained at the end of a long day, she would bounce into my office sharing words of wisdom she learned in one of her new courses. She did accomplish her dream and graduated with an undergraduate degree. Several years ago, she left this life fulfilling her role as a minister and advocate, helping people to fulfill their dreams.

Before she passed away, I asked her what she discovered about herself after returning to school. She told me that she realized her brain was not old; it could still take in new information. She proved that learning never stops, and with faith, you can achieve anything in life.

Many of those women I counseled completed challenging goals filled with obstacles. They had small children to look after, husbands who complained about their wives taking time away from home and were working full-time jobs. They moved forward determined to learn something new. These women uncovered the hidden gems deep inside that were buried for many years.

IT'S YOUR TURN (activity)

LEARN SOMETHING NEW: You, too, may be struggling to find the courage to participate in a career empowerment activity. Round up friends who will support you on your quest and who will not allow you to give up. Ride into the fear.

What is it you want to learn? New learning means taking part in something you enjoy. Has someone reminded you of something you liked doing? The secret to succeeding in learning something new is to remember what author Anthony Robbins has said, "There are no failures, only results." Only after learning something new will you discover new gems inside yourself.

There are no guarantees as to what you'll discover. You may find out you don't like the new activity, and that's OK. It can transition you through a process of elimination. I took a photography class once, and it did not work for me. Was this wasted time? No, it gave me new information about myself, and I learned something new. To this day, my family does not count on me to be the photographer at family events, and that's OK. Don't beat yourself up if your activity does not work. Just keep moving and "Go fetch it" some more.

CHAPTER 3

CREATING A CAREER VISION

> *"Ask for what you want and be prepared to get it."*
>
> *– Dr. Maya Angelou*

Creating a career vision is seeing an image of the career you deserve. This image includes all the new information you've uncovered about yourself through the activities mentioned in the previous chapters. Visualization is an empowerment strategy that will help you create a career vision that communicates your values, strengths and interests.

I discovered visualization techniques after reading Dr. Maxwell Maltz's book, "Psycho-Cybernetic Principals for Creative Living." Dr. Maltz believes that whatever the mind can conceive, the mind can achieve.

I began visualizing my career by asking myself this, "If I could wave a magic wand, what would I see myself doing in the next 10 years?"

My first career visioning experience happened when I was a secondary high school counselor. I loved working with students, but I wanted a career that combined my love of teaching with public speaking.

I read books on career change and met with several career counselors at my alma mater, Temple University. During those career counseling sessions, I discovered that my experience in working with adults at Temple and teaching adults interpersonal communication skills during the summer created a resume that would support securing a position in training and development at a major corporation.

I visualized myself working in a large corporate building in a beautiful large office with a wonderful view of the city. I pictured every single item in my office. I even cut out pictures of a computer and placed them on a board. Then I placed the board in my bedroom to look at every day. (Imagine what my picture of a computer looked like 10 years ago!) I even visualized what a possible workday might look like in my new career.

I learned that cutting out pictures that represent your career vision increases employment opportunities. There were several vision boards on my wall displaying the ultimate dream career. I was very determined to break into the corporate world, but realized how little I knew about corporate training and development.

"What Color is Your Parachute" by Richard Bolles was extremely helpful. This book is still popular today and has been on the bestseller list for almost 10 years. In the book, Bolles suggests an informational interview for those wishing to embark on a new career. This technique helped me achieve my goal of working in the corporate environment. The informational interview felt foreign to me, but I kept moving forward on my career journey.

Setting up the informational interview involved selecting a person who worked in a similar role to the one for which I was searching. This was especially challenging for me because I was not personally acquainted with anyone in the training and development role. Yet, I believe in Divine Order and I believe that there are no accidents in life. If you created a career vision, what you want will appear in your life.

Soon after, I came across a woman I knew many years ago, a dynamic lady who was a senior executive, managing the operations for a large health care facility. We talked about what was happening in our lives and I shared my interest in changing careers. She invited me to her office to share information about her experiences working in a large organization. On the appointed day, I arrived at her office building and rode the elevator to a high floor. This was very different from my school already.

I noticed how beautifully it was decorated; there was a large upholstered couch alongside a large cherry wood desk. I thought, she must be very important because looking out her window brought a spectacular view of the city.

Her office resembled the picture on one of my visioning boards. Then, I got goose bumps when I saw her computer. It was almost identical to the one on my picture board. Smiling to myself, I thought, "So this is what happens when you create a career vision."

During our meeting she shared valuable information about her executive role. While listening to her experiences, I gained clarity on my new career. My vision was being crystallized, not only from hearing more about what I wanted to become, but by actually experiencing the corporate environment.

Visualization strategies are practiced in many different ways.

When people dream about the ultimate car, they visit a showroom. They want to smell the leather, see every detail of the car and imagine driving the vehicle. This is a technique many network marketing distributors use to achieve sales goals.

It's Your Turn: Take a few minutes now and close your eyes. Try to dream about your new career. Create a clear vision down to the finest detail. What are you wearing? Are you in an office or outdoors? What equipment are you using? You may have all the answers instantaneously or you may have to put this book down and think about it for a while.

One of my passions is to read autobiographies of successful people. Through my reading, I've noticed many of them knew their career goals at an early age.

In Viktor Frankl's book, "Man's Search for Meaning," he tells the story of his experiences in concentration camps during World War II. While enduring torture, he envisioned himself lecturing at a podium, relating to students about his experiences. Frankl's vision is what sustained him in the concentration camp, and it enabled him to attain his goal of seeing his wife again.

One evening while sitting at home reading quietly, I received a phone call that affirmed the power of creative visualization. About eight years earlier, early in my consulting career, I was concerned about how children were taught in the urban community. Parents and teachers in several inner city schools complained about the lack of cohesiveness between teachers and students in the elementary schools. Believing passionately that every child deserves to learn in a safe environment, I designed a program that helps teachers learn how to value differences in children. At the time, the school district was embarking on education reform with a new superintendent, and I knew this was an opportunity to market my program.

Joanna Hutton-Hogg and Frederick Bryant, tw
consulting colleagues, supported my passion to
services to the Philadelphia school district. We sp
hours brainstorming and completed the design of
program to help teachers value differences in childre

Trying to secure a contract with the city's school distric,
laborious process. I began to visualize the outcome. I foc,
on working with teachers to help them understand diversi,
issues and safe learning environments, which are classrooms
which differences across race, gender, appearance and other
dimensions are valued.

David P. Richardson, former state representative in Philadelphia,
was my champion in attempting to secure a contract. He
believed in my program and motivated me to climb over the
obstacles to connect with the decision-makers of the school
district. David wrote letters to many key officials and lobbied
the importance of incorporating my program in the schools.

On that evening, David called to say that he had submitted
another letter to the superintendent's office and, hopefully, I
would be hearing from him soon. I appreciated David's support
and had a feeling that the letter may finally find its way to the
superintendent. I didn't give up; my determination and passion
to help children feel valued sharpened my vision to succeed in
securing the contract.

Just when I was beginning to believe there was some hope in
the project, a friend called with the disturbing news that David
suffered a massive heart attack and passed away that very day. I
was devastated.

David was a great friend, not only to me, but also to many
people in Philadelphia. He rarely said "No" to anyone in need
of help or support. He was approachable and down to earth, as

enced by the overflowing numbers of people of all ages
o attended the funeral.

ontinued my quest for David. One evening, not long after,
y phone rang. The caller asked for me by my first name but
ad a different last name. "I think you have the wrong
number," I said. The caller apologized and mentioned that my
voice sounded familiar, and I thought hers did as well.

I said, "Is this Judy?"

"I know who you are now," she said. "I would recall your voice
anywhere. Is this Barbara Moore?"

Moore was my married name at the time. We laughed, and she
said that my phone number was underneath the person's she
intended to call.

Judy and I had not spoken to each other in years. We knew
each other when our children were young, but we drifted apart
over time. We agreed how serendipitous events happen for no
apparent reasons. Then she said, "Wait a minute, we need to
talk about what we are doing in our lives." She was reading
James Redfield's "The Celestine Prophecy," a book that states
there are no accidents in life. Redfield believes there is
significant reason when situations arise that connect people in
unlikely events. Wanting to test her new realization, Judy
suggested that we just talk about what we are doing now, and
see if we connect on anything.

I excitedly agreed, anxious to discover the results of our conversation. I felt like an explorer on a journey of discovering new
opportunities. I couldn't wait to probe our conversation further.

We talked about our children and caught up on old friends; I
told Judy about my new consulting venture and the program I
designed for the Philadelphia school district. I went on to

explain the challenges I'd faced in trying to get my proposal into the right hands. I even mentioned that David was my champion, but that he was no longer here to help me with my quest.

Halfway through my conversation, she interrupted. "This is incredible," she said. "I don't believe this is happening!

"You will never believe who I work with. If you recall, I was a principal in an elementary school when our children were young. Now I have a new position as the new superintendent's special assistant."

We laughed. This felt unreal! But, it was true, and it affirmed that when you envision your dream, the brain moves you to events that lead you closer to that dream.

Following our conversation, a chain of events began to break down the walls of bureaucracy in the Philadelphia school district. Several months later I received my first contract. I thanked God and the universe for connecting me to Judy.

Keeping your vision provides opportunities to make the connections happen. Along the way, barriers will rise up when you least expected. That's life and you must not give up. Norman Vincent Peale in his book, "The Power of Positive Thinking," writes, "Throw your heart over the bar, and the body will follow." He believes that you must use your passion to get beyond the blocks between you and your career journey. With a little faith and a lot of courage, visioning can work for you.

Dr. Maxwell Maltz has said that the brain is like maze. When we set the vision, the brain begins to find the end result. As the brain begins to do its work, you will meet people or receive the information you need to complete your career vision.

IT'S YOUR TURN (activity)

ENVISION YOUR CAREER:

* *Pull together all the information you gathered in "Discovering Your Authenticity"*

* *Visualize every detail of the career.*

* *Cut out pictures and place them on a board or in a picture album.*

* *Look at the pictures frequently or put them in a location that is in your line of vision.*

* *State your intention through prayer, affirmation or meditation.*

* *Claim your divine inheritance of abundance.*

CHAPTER 4

DEVELOPING A CAREER PORTFOLIO

"We don't know who we are until we see what we can do."

— *Martha Grimes*

Now that you have completed career empowerment strategies to discover your authentic self and create a career vision, document all the evidence in a career portfolio. A career portfolio can be a folder, a container or a chest. The portfolio should fit your personality. By now, you should know more about yourself than you did at the beginning of your journey.

The portfolio is filled with positive words that people have said about you in letters, documents or e-mails. You should keep the gems that you found during your journey of self-discovery.

My gems are in folders, envelopes and hidden in a few journals. I look at them when I need to "Go fetch it." Sometimes I have moments of self-doubt and fear; this is part of being human. Looking at my career portfolio gives me strength and acts as a reminder of my authentic self. It allows me to reach into my past to move forward in my journey.

I enjoy saving notes that say something about me that validates my self-discovery. You might think that collecting gems may be self-serving. Don't think of this in a negative way. The empowerment process is self-serving, but it can be a positive affirmation of who you are in this life. Collecting gems is a deliberate act of empowerment.

Some people tend to hide their gems or throw them away. Gems don't clutter. Instead, they add to the joy of discovering the real you. They support you when you hit a few obstacles toward your goal.

I read my gems with gratitude. I thank God for making me. The gems affirm that I am a good person and that I am powerful because I mean something to someone — a child, a student, a daughter, a son or a neighbor. The card says I am a giver to someone, and that may be the information I need to hold onto my journey.

Developing a career portfolio is also helpful in work performance reviews. The performance-evaluation process in corporations assesses and reveals information about your performance. A performance rating determines completion of expected work standards. A merit increase, a raise or a promotion could result from a satisfactory performance review.

In my workshops, participants tell me that they attend performance evaluation meetings with less information than their managers. Managers then control the meeting because they accumulated the data. And, many times, what they collected is not in your favor. Successful performance reviews require you to bring accurate data on your work experiences. The career portfolio is an empowerment tool that helps you to partner in controlling the performance review meeting. Being armed with positive information during the meeting is critical to help the manager understand your strengths. It is unrealistic to expect managers to know everything about you. The information in your portfolio is your evidence of who you are and your contributions.

Once, while facilitating an "It's Your Turn" seminar at a conference in San Francisco, I met up with Denise, a participant in one of my prior workshops. After that workshop, Denise decided to create a Career Portfolio to assist herself in interviewing for an executive promotion in her organization.

Denise gathered the results of her inner work on self-discovery and past achievements in the organization. She incorporated the information in her Career Portfolio and gave a presentation in the job interview. The interviewer was impressed with her ability to articulate her talents and skills.

Denise said she was convinced that the Career Portfolio technique helped her to get the promotion. Denise courageously did her inner work and can now move forward with an awareness of her authentic identity.

When I was a manager of training and development in a large health care organization, I met people who were devalued during performance review meetings. These negative experiences impacted their lives greatly. They went into a review knowing they completed work expectations and achieved bottom-line results, but they left feeling undervalued. This can be devastating. Good performance reviews are indicative of managers who are trained or inherently know how to reward and monitor performance.

IT'S YOUR TURN (activity)

GATHER EVIDENCE: Go to your next performance review meeting with a list of your strengths, talents and accomplishments, even if it isn't required. Evidences of your accomplishments at work come in different forms. They can be certificates of accomplishments from training programs you attended or complimentary letters from co-workers or managers on a task you achieved.

If you do not have any evidence of your accomplished tasks, empower yourself by asking people who worked with you to write a letter confirming your accomplishments. No one will make a career portfolio happen for you.

If you are in charge of a church project, save the flier from the event. Ask people to complete an evaluation about your performance. Save the comments that affirm your planning skills. This is evidence of who you are and the skills you possess.

Developing a career portfolio is an empowerment strategy that acknowledges that you are worthy. Not only do you believe it within yourself, but you also have written proof. Whether you work in a large corporation or a small company, this empowerment strategy is critical in seeking a new career within or outside your organization, or starting your own business.

If you want a promotion, keep written information on your career progress to empower you to take more control of the performance appraisal process. Many times we are victims of managers who dictate what they know and what they have observed about your progress instead of you creating a partnership in documenting your progress. It is imperative that you bring something to the performance meeting that outlines who you are in the organization.

CHAPTER 5

NETWORKING, NETWORKING, NETWORKING

"You know what real power is? Real power is when you are doing exactly what you are supposed to be doing the best it can be done. Authentic power. There's a surge, there's a kind of energy field that says, 'I'm in my groove. I'm in my groove.' And nobody has to tell you, 'You go, girl,' because, you know, you're already gone.

– Oprah Winfrey

By now, you should have a better idea of what you are supposed to be doing in life. If not, take the time to keep working toward finding the real you. Don't stop. Enjoy accessing your authentic self.

In the meantime, begin putting who you are into the universe. The people you need to help you become authentic are waiting to be discovered. This can happen if you network, network, network.

I helped people network when I was teaching in higher education. One of the course requirements for my MBA students was career counseling. Upon completing the MBA degree, many students wanted to change careers or move up, taking advantage of upward mobility in the corporate environment. Unfortunately, obtaining an MBA or any other degree does not guarantee a career promotion, nor does it make the change in careers an easy process. Many recruiters in major corporations say the want ads are the least likely way of getting a job, and believe that networking can create more opportunities in meeting business contacts.

Networking requires a desire and passion to create the career you deserve. Completing the Career Empowerment Strategies mentioned in the four previous chapters helps to give you the energy to put the next step into active motion.

Networking creates serendipitous events. You may not understand how it happens when you meet one person who connects you to your career vision, but it is important to acknowledge the experience and act on it.

I have counseled people who have sabotaged their career dreams when they neglected the opportunity to network. Fear and doubt sets in, and foundation building is aborted before the opportunity has a chance to take effect. It's like experiencing a fear of success. "I can't believe I am meeting this person who really is going to help me with my dream," they think. Panic sets in and they freeze. But they are back to where they started — wishing, hoping and dreaming.

Networking is the experience that shows you are ready for action. You have done your work. You know who you are and your vision is clear. You are empowered to make the career success happen.

When I changed careers from education to business, I did not understand the corporate world. I loved teaching, but raising two daughters as a single parent meant increasing my income to pay for college tuition. Several of my friends worked for major corporations and were making more money than my teaching salary. To increase my income, I developed workshops for women in assertiveness training during the summer. In addition, I facilitated interpersonal communication skills workshops. My experience in working with adults in higher education paid off in changing careers.

Making the decision to leave education and work in a corporate environment was difficult. My knowledge and acquaintances in the business sector were limited. My working experience was focused on contacts with people in education.

In the Chapter 3, I wrote about how one of my informational interviews was with a friend who was a senior vice president in a major health care organization. I used that interview to help me change careers. Her information was extremely valuable, and it provided me with information about the culture of the business world. I also received an image of a real corporate office.

During several information interviews, I was asked to leave a copy of my resume. I found that people were interested in my career plans. Someone once said that networking happens when preparedness meets opportunity. I was prepared, did my homework, read career books, examined my skills and networked with people in the business world.

Examples of the types of questions to ask during informational interviews can be found in Katharine Hansen's book, "A Foot in the Door" or the previously mentioned "What Color is Your Parachute."

Networking may seem intimidating to people who think they are shy or have challenging social skills. But this is the time to stretch and have faith that you can network. Create a support group of friends and talk about your fears in meeting new people. Remember, you worked hard on the first four steps to empower yourself to create the career you deserve. Don't stop now. Do whatever it takes to get started.

I am certified in Myers Briggs Type Indicator (MBTI). MBTI is an instrument that assesses your personality type. One of the outcomes of MBTI is to understand where you get your energy, which falls under extrovert or introvert. The basic premise of MBTI grounded Carl Jung's principle that differences are good not bad. If you are an introvert, it is not bad or a character flaw; you just prefer to get your energy from within.

And, likely, networking is not your favorite activity. This doesn't mean you do not like to socialize with people; you just prefer to work with someone one-on-one. You may prefer to read a book about networking before you explore meeting someone. You may not uncomfortable talking about yourself. In "A Foot in the Door," Katherine Hansen says, "Networking doesn't mean asking everyone you run into if he or she knows where the job openings are. It means establishing relationships so that you can enlist support and comfortably ask for ideas, advice and referrals of those with hiring power."

IT'S YOUR TURN (activity)

NETWORK NOW:

- *Have your business cards ready to give out. Being prepared to meet the opportunity is key.*

- *Have an attitude of not what can you get out of the experience, but what can you give back. Keep an attitude of gratitude. When you meet someone, ask is there something you can give in return. The principle of cause and effect is that when you give, you receive. Just taking and not giving in a networking experience limits the opportunity for more connections to happen in your life.*

- *Attend professional organizations in the area of career interests. You will find many of these organizations listed in business magazines. Select one that works for you. Find out the time and place where meetings are held. Keep an open mind when you go. George C. Fraser, author of "Success Runs in Our Race: The Complete Guide to Networking in the African American Community and Race for Success," is widely known for being an expert in networking. Fraser believes that African Americans should be empowered to be successful because we are historically strong people. You might want to review the list of networking organizations listed yearly in magazines, like Black Enterprise or Inc. Of course, the Internet is a valuable resource for networking.*

You cannot fail by attending a networking event. Failure doesn't happen; only results happen.

- *Follow-up with your contacts. I know collecting business cards over a period of time can create stacks stuffed in a desk drawer. Don't let that happen. When someone gives you a business card with a gift of a new contact, information or just a keep-in-touch tone, write on the back of the card where you met, the gift and what you are giving back. Contact them the following week, because a missed opportunity diminishes the cause-and-effect process. Keep the energy moving; one connection leads to another connection.*

Many times while traveling, I meet people who give me ideas for a book or just new information that helps me in my work. I enjoy meeting new people because I strongly believe that my vision for success is in the universe. I just show up and let the world give me what I need to take action.

On one of my frequent visits to Cape May, N.J., I was staying at my favorite Bed and Breakfast, "Akwaaba by the Sea." My husband and I frequently stay there because the innkeepers, Monique and Glen, are so special. In addition, we have met the most fantastic people at Akwaaba. I am proud to say our wedding was the first wedding held there.

Shopping is one of my favorite things to do in Cape May, and on this particular visit, one of my goals was to find the perfect earrings to match a dress I was wearing to a wedding. A store kept coming up in my mind that my daughter had told me about, but I could not find it that day. My daughter was out of town so I decided to just let Spirit guide me. I kept telling my husband, after looking at many stores and not finding these earrings, I must find the store. I left him sitting patiently on one of the mall benches and started on my journey. I went down a small street and looked up a familiar name. I wasn't sure if this was the store, but I walked in and found a woman behind the counter with an approachable smile.

She offered to help me find earrings, and during our conversation, while testing out different styles and colors, I noticed her incredible artistic ability to mix and match colors. Our conversation then focused on her main career as an artist. That then led to mentioning my father as an animator and how I would love to tell his story.

To make a long story short, the result of that meeting led to her referring me to a wonderful educational organization she believed would be interested in learning more about my father.

When I returned home, my new connection sent me an e-mail, saying she followed up and made the connection for me. I made the call and am now preparing to send them information. The rest is yet to follow.

Networking takes on many forms. When your goals are clear and your vision is focused on what you want to happen, watch how events unfold. It just takes creating your intention and letting the universe guide you to the source. Trust me, it works if you believe that it can.

CONCLUSION

" We need to find the courage to say no to the things and people
that are not serving us if we want to rediscover ourselves and
live our lives with authenticity.

– Barbara De Angelis

By now, you may be wondering if all this work is worth it to
find your career path. Try this activity to help you put all this
work in perspective.

IT'S YOUR TURN (activity)

WHAT'S NEXT: Get a blank sheet of paper and draw a straight
line across the middle of the page.

On the left end of the line, write your birth date. Write your
current age in the middle of the line. On the extreme right of
the line, write the age to which you want to live. Subtract the
age you are now from the age you wrote for your passing.
Circle the number. This number defines how many years you

want to live "God willing", as they say.

It really doesn't matter what number you placed. What is important is that this number represents a certain amount of time. It demands the question, "What do you plan to do with these remaining years?" This exercise awakens you to see that you have ample number of years to create the life you want.

No one likes to think of death. Fear of dying is one of the most daunting fears. But you will not live forever. So, what will you do with all these years left? If you plan to retire, that's fine, but what will you do when you retire? Today, a large population of baby boomers will live past 70 years of age.

It is not unusual to have three careers in a lifetime. My father, Tee Collins, returned to school at age 60 to receive his master's degree in computer animation, and was the first animator on Sesame Street. In the pilot segment, my father designed the letter "W" for Wanda the Witch. After closing his animation and film studio in New York City, he was approached by Ohio University to teach animation. He remained at Ohio University for three years before being recruited by the University of Central Florida to teach animation there. He taught for 11 years until his passing in 2000.

My father loved teaching and this explains my love of teaching. I believe many times our talents and skills are passed on to us from our parents. He was my role model for doing the work he enjoyed and following his purpose in life.

I believe strongly that empowerment means controlling what you want in life. Destiny is a word of choice if you believe that life creates what will happen to you. The flip side to destiny is intention. Intention dictates what you intend to do with your life. Therefore, intention to me means doing my inner work. It means you should "go fetch" what you need to find out more about you, create the vision, set goals and network to be open to universal possibilities.

I am a baby boomer who feels like I am in my 30s. My attitude is to act like I want, be energetic, seek the best in me and have fun living out my life.

I heard motivational speaker Wayne Dyer once say that his teacher, psychologist Abraham Maslow, had said that self-actualized people are people who live to their fullest potential. What I believe he meant was that we must constantly seek what we can become. Yes, it takes work. But, I am worth it.

My daughter once gave me a gift that sits on my desk. It's a sculpture of a woman soaking in a bathtub filled with bubbles. The inscription reads, "You yourself, as much as anybody in the entire universe, deserve your love and affection. — The Buddha.

It's Your Turn to realize that you do too.

About the Author

Dr. Barbara R. Collins, management development consultant, executive coach, professor, keynote speaker and author, began her career as an educator. She started as an elementary school teacher in Philadelphia, teaching fourth grade and later becoming a high school guidance counselor. Barbara was passionate about teaching and working with students.

However, as a divorced and single parent, she left education to increase her income. Barbara entered the corporate world as a human resources development manager at Independence Blue Cross in Philadelphia, where during her 11 years she designed and implemented training programs for more than 1,400 employees. Barbara later was employed as an organizational development internal consultant, assisting in the Corporate Wide, Total Quality and Diversity Culture Change initiative at Core States Financial, also in Philadelphia.

Barbara's parents instilled in her the importance of education at an early age. She received her bachelor's degree in Science from Cheyney State University, in Cheyney, PA, and master's degree in Education, specializing in Counseling Psychology, from Antioch University, in Yellow Springs, OH, and her doctorate in Group and Organizational Behavior from Temple University, also in Philadelphia.

During Barbara's 20-plus years in business, she created her own consulting company, Positive Trends, Inc., which specializes in helping organizations develop and implement strategic initiatives to enhance work productivity and achieve organizational goals. Barbara helped numerous clients maximize people differences to accomplish business goals, manage change in a changing environment and learn effective team group process strategies. Barbara's clients have included the Philadelphia Department of Public Health, Philadelphia Water Department, University of Pennsylvania Health System, New York State Council on the Arts, PECO Energy, Philadelphia School District, Pennsylvania Convention Center and numerous others. Her keynote presentations have been given to the 11th Annual CITR Conference, Consortium of Information and Telecommunications Executives, Inc., Bell Atlantic, School District of Philadelphia, POWA (Professional Women of Antigua-Barbuda), Women in Transportation Services and Jack and Jill, Inc.-Philadelphia Chapter and many more.

While working in education and business, Barbara began her journey of self-discovery. Today, Barbara's life has transformed from what she had to do into doing what she loves and what feels authentically right. She is working in her dharma, a feeling of timelessness. Her inner search during the past 20 years has taken her on a wonderful and exciting journey of self-discovery that finds her a TV and print commercial actor, associate professor, professional keynote speaker and executive life coach.

Today, she dedicates her work to helping women find their authentic self. Barbara realized many years ago that finding our Divine purpose takes work and proactive planning; it doesn't just happen or fall into our laps.

To help Barbara proactively build her new career as a keynote speaker and coach, she created her own personal board of directors. Barbara incorporates a synergistic approach to remain authentic in working with women. H.G. Chissel, well-known Feng Shui consultant, along with Ginni Stiles, professional organizer, helps Barbara to be clear about her intentions both in her personal and professional life, and assists her in building an organized infrastructure. Barbara's award-winning web designer, David Kaneda, is part of her team to ensure that the communication to women is congruent with the goals in building the foundation for "It's Your Turn."

As an active member of the National Speakers Association (4,000 members), and NSA's Mid-Atlantic Speakers Association, she has a proven track record as a speaker to varied audiences. Currently, her board memberships include The Arts and Spirituality Center, a multi-faith, multicultural organization whose mission is to facilitate healing, empowerment and transformation of individuals and communities through spiritual and creative expression, as well as the Sisters Health Initiative (SHI)-Women of Color, working to decrease breast cancer risk factors. Barbara is also a member of the National Coalition of 100 Black Women and The Society, Inc., a non-profit organization committed to providing opportunities for the development of the fine and performing arts for youth, with special emphasis on African-American youth.

For more information about Dr. Collins please contact:

Dr. Barbara R. Collins
Positive Trends, Inc.
P.O. Box 27, Skippack, PA 19474-9998
Voice: 610-409-8905
Fax: 610-409-8902
www.drbarbaracollins.com
positivetrends@comcast.net

To schedule a **free 30-minute consultation** on her website, visit www.drbarbaracollins.com and click on "Send Me A Message."